'. . . I'll stop doing it as soon as I understand what I'm doing.'

D0676202

PLATO

Born *c.* 424 BC, Athens, Greece
Died *c.* 347 BC, Athens, Greece

The account was written following Socrates' trial in 399 BC
and is taken from *The Last Days of Socrates*.

PLATO IN PENGUIN CLASSICS

Republic
The Last Days of Socrates
The Laws
Phaedrus
Protagoras and Meno
Timaeus and Critias
Theaetetus
Early Socratic Dialogues
The Symposium
Gorgias

PLATO

Socrates' Defence

Translated by
Christopher Rowe

PENGUIN BOOKS

PENGUIN CLASSICS

Published by the Penguin Group
Penguin Books Ltd, 80 Strand, London WC2R 0RL, England
Penguin Group (USA) Inc., 375 Hudson Street, New York, New York 10014, USA
Penguin Group (Canada), 90 Eglinton Avenue East, Suite 700, Toronto, Ontario,
Canada M4P 2Y3 (a division of Pearson Penguin Canada Inc.)
Penguin Ireland, 25 St Stephen's Green, Dublin 2, Ireland
(a division of Penguin Books Ltd)
Penguin Group (Australia), 707 Collins Street, Melbourne, Victoria 3008, Australia
(a division of Pearson Australia Group Pty Ltd)
Penguin Books India Pvt Ltd, 11 Community Centre, Panchsheel Park,
New Delhi – 110 017, India
Penguin Group (NZ), 67 Apollo Drive, Rosedale, Auckland 0632, New Zealand
(a division of Pearson New Zealand Ltd)
Penguin Books (South Africa) (Pty) Ltd, Block D, Rosebank Office Park,
181 Jan Smuts Avenue, Parktown North, Gauteng 2193, South Africa

Penguin Books Ltd, Registered Offices: 80 Strand, London WC2R 0RL, England

www.penguin.com

This edition published in Penguin Classics 2015
002

Translation and editorial material copyright © Christopher Rowe, 2010

The moral right of the translator has been asserted

Set in 10/14.5 pt Baskerville 10 Pro
Typeset by Jouve (UK), Milton Keynes
Printed in Great Britain by Clays Ltd, St Ives plc

A CIP catalogue record for this book is available from the British Library

ISBN: 978-0-141-39764-1

www.greenpenguin.co.uk

MIX
Paper from
responsible sources
FSC
www.fsc.org   FSC™ C018179

Penguin Books is committed to a sustainable
future for our business, our readers and our planet.
This book is made from Forest Stewardship
Council™ certified paper.

Socrates' Defence

I don't know what effect my accusers have had on you, men of Athens, but I can tell you they almost made even me forget where I was, so convincingly did they speak. But when it comes to the truth, they've said virtually nothing. The most astounding of the many lies they told came when they claimed that you needed to take care not to be deceived by me, because of my artfulness as a speaker. Their lack of concern that their claim will immediately be proved false, as I display my total lack of artfulness as a speaker, seemed to me more shameful than anything else – unless, of course, 'artful speaker' is what these people call someone who tells the truth; because if that's what they have in mind, I'll admit to being an orator, and one in a different league from them. In any case, I repeat, they've said either little or nothing that's true, whereas you'll hear from me the whole truth. What you won't hear from me at all, I swear to you by Zeus, men of Athens, is language like theirs, full of fine words and phrases and arranged in due order. What you will hear will be in the words that come to me at the time, and as they come to me, since I'm confident that what I say is just. Let none of you expect any more. It wouldn't be fitting in any case for someone of my age, Athenians, to come before you and fiddle with words like an adolescent boy. But if there is one thing I ask of you, men of Athens, it's that if you hear me talking, in my defence, in the same language I habitually use in the marketplace around the bankers' stalls (where many of you have heard me) and elsewhere, you shouldn't be astonished or protest at it. This is the way it is: this is the first time, in my seventy years, that I've come before a law-court, and so the way people talk here is simply alien to me. So just as, if I were actually an alien, you'd obviously be sympathetic to me if I spoke in the same kind of Greek and the same style that I'd been brought up to speak, so I ask you here and now (and it's a just request, at least as I see it) to disregard the manner of my delivery – perhaps it won't stand comparison, perhaps it will – and to consider just this, and give your minds to this alone:

whether or not what I say is just. For that is what makes for excellence in a juryman, just as what makes an excellent orator is telling the truth.

Well, then, the right thing for me to do first, men of Athens, is to defend myself against the first false accusations made against me, and my first accusers, leaving till after that the accusations and accusers that have come along later. The fact is that it's nothing new for you Athenians to hear accusations against me; plenty of people have made them for plenty of years now, without saying anything that's true. Those accusers are the ones I fear more than Anytus and his lot, frightening though these latter ones are; more frightening, Athenians, are the ones who've been filling the ears of most of you since you were children and trying to convince you of something that's not the slightest bit truer than the rest: that there's a Socrates around who's an expert – one who dabbles in theories about the heavenly bodies, who's already searched out everything beneath the earth and who makes the weaker argument the stronger. It's the people spreading accusations like these, men of Athens, that are genuinely frightening. Why? Because their audience thinks that people who conduct research into these things don't even believe

3

in the gods. There are also a large number of these accusers, and they've been making their accusations for a long time; what's more they were already talking to you at an age when you would have most readily believed them, being children, some of you, or adolescents, and they were prosecuting a case that went by default because there was no one there to defend it. But what is most unreasonable of all is that even their names aren't available to be listed, unless, that is, one or another of them happens to be a comic writer. The ones who have slandered me out of malice and convinced you of their slanders, and the ones who, having been convinced themselves, have gone on to convince others – all these accusers are the most difficult to deal with, because it isn't even possible to have them appear in court, or to cross-examine a single one of them; I must simply shadow-box my defence against them, as it were, and mount my cross-examination with no one there to answer me. So I ask you to accept that, as I say, my accusers are twofold: apart from the ones who have spoken out recently, there are these other, more long-standing accusers I'm talking of, and I ask you to join me in supposing that I must defend myself first against the latter sort – for you yourselves heard them making their accusations earlier, and you were exposed to them much more than to these later accusers.

So, then: defend myself I must, men of Athens, and attempt to remove from your minds, in this short time allotted to me, the slander that you have been exposed to for so long. Well, that's what I would like to achieve, if it's in any way the better outcome whether for you or for me. I would like to have some sort of success in my defence. But I think it's going to be hard, and I'm well aware what kind of task it is. Never mind; let it go as it pleases the god, and meanwhile the law must be obeyed and a defence made.

Let's start, then, from the beginning, by asking what the accusation is that lies at the root of all the slander on which I suppose Meletus must be relying in taking out the present indictment against me. Well, then: what did the slanderers actually say when they slandered me? I should read it out, as if it were the prosecutors' affidavit: 'Socrates is guilty of busying himself with research into what's beneath the earth and in the heavens and making the weaker argument the stronger and teaching the same things to others.' That's the sort of thing that's in my pretend affidavit: you saw it for yourselves in Aristophanes' comedy – a 'Socrates' being whirled around above the stage, claiming he's 'walking on air' and uttering a whole lot of other nonsense about things of which, speaking for myself, I have no inkling whatsoever. Nor do I say this out of disrespect for such knowledge, if there's someone around with expertise in such matters (please let me not have to defend myself against another suit brought by Meletus!); the simple fact is, men of Athens, that I have nothing to do with these things. As witnesses, I offer you yourselves, or most of you: I ask those of you who've ever heard me in conversation (and there are plenty of you who have) to tell the others, if any one of you has ever yet heard me making the smallest mention of such things, and then you'll be in a position to see that the same also holds good for all the other things that people in general say about me.

In fact not only is none of these things true, but also, if you've heard from any source that I undertake to teach people and charge money for it – that's not true either, though I think it would be a fine thing if someone did turn out to be able to teach people, like Gorgias of Leontini, or Prodicus of Ceos, or Hippias of Elis. Each of these individuals, Athenians, is able to go into one city after another and persuade her young men, who have the option of spending time with whichever of their own fellow citizens they wish for no charge at all, to get together with *them* instead and not only pay good money for it but be grateful to them as well. Indeed I've learned there's another expert, a Parian, who's here in Athens at the moment. As it happened, I recently went up to someone who's paid out more money to sophists than everyone else put together, Callias son of Hipponicus, and I asked him – he has two sons – 'Callias, if your two sons had been born colts or calves, we could find someone to hire to take charge of them and make them fine and good, equipped with the appropriate excellence; and this person would be an expert in horse-training or farming. But as it is, since the two of them are human beings, whom do you have in mind to put in charge of them? Who is expert in this sort of excellence – the human, citizen sort? I imagine, seeing that you've acquired sons, that you've looked into the question. Is there anyone like this,' I said, 'or not?' 'Yes, absolutely,' he said. I asked 'Who is it? Where does he come from? And how much does he charge for his teaching?' 'It's Evenus, Socrates,' he said; 'he's from Paros, and he charges five minas.' My reaction was to call Evenus a fortunate man if he genuinely possessed this expertise, and teaches it at so low a price. I'd certainly be preening myself and putting on all sorts of airs if I had this knowledge. But the fact is that I don't, men of Athens.

One of you will probably then interject 'But Socrates, what is it about you? Where have these slanders against you come from? So much gossip and talk can't have come about because you were up to nothing more extraordinary than anyone else; you must be doing something different from what ordinary people do. So tell us what it is, so that we don't get things wrong about you in the way others do.' Now *this* seems to me a legitimate thing to say, and I will try to show you just what it is that has brought about the false reputation that I have. So hear me out. Probably some of you will think I'm not being serious; but I can assure you that what I'm going to say will be the whole truth. I have earned my reputation, men of Athens, for no reason other than that I possess a certain sort of wisdom. What sort of wisdom could this be? Probably a wisdom of a human sort. It's likely enough that I really am wise in this way; whereas those others I mentioned just now will be wise with a sort of wisdom that's beyond the human – or if that's not so, I don't know what to say, because *I* certainly don't have their wisdom, and anyone who says I do is lying and deliberately misrepresenting me.

Now please don't protest, men of Athens, even if I may seem to you to be boasting a bit. What I say won't be coming from me; it comes from a source you'll find impeccable. As to my ... well, as to whether it actually *is* wisdom, and what sort of wisdom it is, as witness I mean to offer you: the god at Delphi. How so? I imagine you know Chaerephon. He was not only a friend of mine from my youth, but a friend of the people, who shared your recent exile and returned from exile with you. You also know what kind of person Chaerephon was, and how single-minded he was about anything he undertook. This time he actually went to Delphi and had the face to ask the oracle (once again, Athenians, I ask you not to protest) – he actually asked whether anyone was wiser than I was, and the Pythia duly replied that there was no one wiser. Chaerephon's brother here will testify to all this, since the man himself is dead.

Consider why I'm telling you this: to explain to you the source of the slander against me. When I heard what the Pythia had said, I thought to myself 'What can the god be saying? It's a riddle: what can it mean? I've no knowledge of my being wise in any respect, great or small, so what is he saying when he claims that I'm the wisest? He certainly can't be *lying*; that's out of the question for him.' For a long time I was at a loss as to what the god was saying, but then, with great reluctance, I turned to inquiring into his response. I went about it like this: I approached one of those individuals people suppose to be wise, on the basis that here if anywhere I could challenge the oracle's response by pointing out someone it had missed – 'This person here is wiser than me, and you said I was wiser than him!' Well, I examined this person – I've no need to mention his name, but the person with whom I had the sort of experience I'm about to describe, when I examined him, was one of the political experts; and as I conversed with him, I formed the conclusion that, while this person seemed wise to lots of other people, and especially to himself, in reality he wasn't; upon which I made a concerted attempt to demonstrate to him that he only thought he was wise, but really wasn't. Well, that made him hate me, as it did a lot of those who were present; but

I reasoned to myself, as I left him, like this – 'I am actually wiser than this person; likely enough neither of us knows anything of importance, but he *thinks* he knows something when he doesn't, whereas just as I don't know anything, so I don't think I do, either. So I appear to be wiser, at least than him, in just this one small respect: that when I don't know things, I don't think that I do either.' After that I went on to someone else, supposedly wiser than him, and reached exactly the same conclusion; at that point I became an object of hate both for him and for many others.

Well, after that I went on to another person, and another; distressed and fearful though I was as I perceived their hatred for me, I thought I must make my business with the god the first priority. So, as I searched for the meaning of the oracle, there was nothing for it but to approach everyone with a reputation for knowing something. And by the Dog, men of Athens, because I'm bound to tell you the truth, I swear to you that it turned out something like this: that those with the greatest reputations seemed to me, as I continued my divinely instigated search, practically the most deficient, while others who were supposedly inferior seemed better endowed when it came to good sense.

I should give you a picture of these wanderings of mine – these labours, as it were, that I undertook in order to leave the oracle's response unrefuted. After the political experts I went on to the poets – tragic, dithyrambic and the rest – on the basis that it was here I'd catch myself red-handed, as actually more ignorant than them. So, picking out those of their poetic compositions they seemed to me to have spent most effort on, I would ask them what they were trying to say, with a view to learning a thing or two from them as well. Well, Athenians, I blush to tell you the truth, but it has to be told: practically speaking, almost everyone present would have better things to say than they did about their own compositions. So I quickly came to the same conclusion about the poets as I had about the others, that it wasn't through wisdom that they did what they did, but rather through some sort of natural talent, or because they were inspired like the seers and the soothsayers, who make many fine utterances but have no knowledge about the things they're saying. That, I thought, was clearly the case with the poets too; and I noticed that they thought their poetry-making also made them the wisest of men about everything else too, which they weren't. So I left the poets thinking

that I'd outdone them in the same respect that I'd outdone the political experts. Finally, I went on to the
craftsmen. I knew that I myself had practically no
knowledge, whereas I knew that I'd find them knowing
lots of fine things. Nor was I mistaken about that. They
did know things I didn't, and in that respect they were
wiser than me. But, men of Athens, the good craftsmen
too seemed to me to suffer from the same failing as the
poets: because they were accomplished in practising
their skill, each one of them claimed to be wisest about
other things too, the most important ones at that – and
this error of theirs seemed to me to obscure the wisdom
they did possess. The outcome was that I asked myself,
in defence of the oracle, whether I'd prefer to be as I
am, and not be either in the least bit wise with their
wisdom or ignorant with their ignorance, or to have
both their wisdom and their ignorance together. And
the answer I gave myself, and the oracle, was that I was
better off as I was.

The result of my inquiry, then, men of Athens, has
been that I have become an object of hatred for many
people, and hatred of a particularly intractable and
intolerable kind, which has brought about numerous
slanders against me and given me that reputation of

being *wise*; for on every occasion the onlookers suppose that if I refute someone else I must myself be an expert in whatever the discussion is about. But the truth most likely is, Athenians, that it's the god who's really wise, and that in this utterance of the oracle he's simply saying that human wisdom is worth very little, or nothing at all. And in mentioning this 'Socrates', he appears to be using my name just to treat me as an illustration – as if he were to say 'The wisest among you, humans, is the one who like Socrates has recognized that in truth he's worth nothing when it comes to wisdom.' That's why I, for my part, still go around even now on this search of mine, instigated by the god, so that if I think anyone, whether fellow citizen or foreigner, might be wise, I'll sniff him out; and whenever I conclude that he isn't wise, I come to the aid of the god by demonstrating that he isn't. It's because of this preoccupation of mine that I've not had the leisure to make any contribution worth speaking of either to the city's affairs or to my own; instead I find myself in extreme poverty, because of my service to the god.

In addition to all of this the young ones follow me around, since they have all the leisure in the world – that is, the wealthiest of them, and they do it of their own accord, because they love hearing those fellows being put to the test; often they copy me amongst themselves, and then they go on to try out their technique by examining others, and I imagine that as a result they find a great superfluity of people who think they know something but actually know little or nothing. So the next thing is that their victims get angry with me instead of with themselves, and talk about some quite abominable Socrates who corrupts the young; and when anyone asks them what they have against him, and what he teaches that has this effect, they have nothing to say and simply don't know; but so as to avoid seeming to be at a loss they produce the slogans that are ready to hand for use against all philosophers: 'things up in the heavens and below the earth', 'not believing in the gods', 'making the weaker argument the stronger'. They wouldn't want to admit the truth, which is that they're shown up by their questioners as pretending to know when they actually know nothing. So because of what I take to be their desire to get ahead, their vigour, and their sheer numbers, and because they talk so earnestly and convincingly about me, they've managed to fill your ears from way back with an equally vigorous slander. On the back of all of this, Meletus has now joined in the attack on me, along with Anytus and Lycon: Meletus out of irritation on behalf of the poets, Anytus on behalf of the craftsmen and the political experts, and Lycon on behalf of the orators. So, as I was saying at the beginning, I'd be astonished if I turned out to be able to remove all this slander from your minds in so short a time, when you have been exposed to it for so long. What I'm telling you, men of Athens, is the truth, and I address you without concealing anything, significant or not, and without dissimulation. But that's the reason, I'm pretty sure, that I'm so hated; and that in itself is proof that I'm right, and that the slanders against me and their causes are as I have described them. No matter whether you look into the matter now or later, that's what you'll find.

Let this, then, be a sufficient defence before you in relation to the charges made against me by my first accusers; next I shall try to defend myself against Meletus – good, patriotic Meletus, as he represents himself – and the other later accusers.

Let's do as we did before, then; let's read their affidavit, as if it belonged to a different set of accusers. It's something like this; it says that Socrates is guilty of corrupting the young and not believing in the gods the city believes in, but in other new divinities. So the charge is like that. Let's examine each aspect of this charge, one by one.

The man says I'm guilty of corrupting the young. But I say, men of Athens, that it's Meletus who's the guilty party, for treating serious matters as a joke – taking people to court as if it were a light matter, and pretending a serious concern for things that never meant anything to him up till now. I'll try to demonstrate to you that this is so.

[*There follows a period of cross-examination.*]

Here, Meletus, and tell me this: am I right in saying it's your first priority that the younger among us should be in the best possible condition?

'It is.'

So come on, tell these people: who is it that makes them better? Plainly you must know, since it means so much to you. At any rate you've found the person who's corrupting them, as you claim, namely me, and you're bringing him before these jurymen here and charging him; so who's the one to make them better? Come on, say who it is; reveal to them who it is. – Do you see, Meletus? You say nothing, because you've nothing *to* say. But doesn't that seem to you to be shameful, and already sufficient proof of exactly what I'm saying, that it's not a meaningful subject to you? Fine. So tell me, my good man, who makes our young ones better people?

'It's the laws.'

That wasn't what I was asking, my fine fellow; I was asking you what *person* makes them better – someone who knows these very things, the laws, above anything else.

'These people here, Socrates, the members of the jury.'

What are you saying, Meletus? These people are able to teach the young, make them better?

'Certainly.'

All of them? Or just some of them, and not others?

'All of them.'

A happy answer, by Hera; you're saying there's a great superfluity of people to help them. What about the spectators over there – do they make the young better as well, or not?

'They do too.'

What about the members of the Council?

'The Councillors too.'

Surely, then, Meletus, those who sit in the Assembly, the Assemblymen – *they* don't corrupt the younger ones? All of these make them better too?

'They do too.'

In that case, Meletus, it seems that every single Athenian makes them into fine and upstanding people except for me; I alone corrupt them. Is that what you're saying?

'That's what I'm saying, most emphatically.'

What great misfortune you've condemned me to! Answer me this: does it seem to you to be like this with horses too? That it's all mankind that improves them, and just one person who corrupts them? Or is the situation quite the opposite of this, that there's one person or a very small number of people who can improve them, namely the horse-experts, whereas most people, if they even have anything to do with horses, or use them, actually make them worse? Isn't that how it is, Meletus, whether with horses or with any other sort of animal? Yes indeed it is, whether you and Anytus deny it or accept it; because if there's one person and only one who corrupts our young men, while everyone else benefits them, it would be a great piece of good fortune in their case. But the fact is,

Meletus, that your behaviour is sufficient demonstration of your total lack of concern for the young up till now; you clearly show your own negligence, and the fact that the things you're bringing me to court for aren't a meaningful subject for you at all.

And answer for me this further question, for heaven's sake, Meletus: is it better to live among fellow citizens who are good or those who are vicious? Sir, answer the question – it's not a difficult one. Don't vicious people do some sort of damage to those closest to them, in whatever context, whereas good people correspondingly do them some sort of good?

'Yes, absolutely.'

Well, is there anyone who prefers to be damaged rather than benefited by the people he has to deal with? Answer, my good man, since the law says you must. Is there anyone who wishes to be damaged?

'Certainly not.'

Come on, then: are you bringing me before the court for corrupting the young and making them more vicious intentionally or unintentionally?

'Intentionally.'

What's this, Meletus? Are you so much wiser than me, even though you're so young and I'm so old, that you've noticed that the bad always do some damage to those who are nearest to them and the good benefit them, whereas *I* have reached such a pitch of ignorance that I'm actually unaware of the fact that if I make anyone among the people I associate with into a depraved person, I shall very likely be the recipient of some damage from him? You're telling me I'm intentionally doing something *that* bad? You don't convince me that I am, and I don't think you'll convince anyone else in the world, either. Either I don't corrupt people, or, if I do, I corrupt them unintentionally, so that whichever way you take it your charge is false. And if I do corrupt people unintentionally, then the law is that for such offences a person shouldn't be brought to court; instead he should be taken off for private instruction and a private telling off, since evidently, if I'm acting unintentionally, I'll stop doing it as soon as I understand what I'm doing. But you shied away from getting together with me to give me my lesson; you refused that option and preferred to bring me to court, when the law says prosecution is for those needing punishment, not lecturing.

So there it is, men of Athens: what I was claiming, that Meletus has never yet concerned himself in the slightest degree with these things, is by now clear enough. But all the same tell us *how* you say I corrupt the younger among us, Meletus. Or is it, clearly, to go by the indictment as you've framed it, by teaching them not to believe in the gods the city believes in but to treat new and different things as 'divine'? Isn't that what you say I teach and so corrupt them?

'Yes, absolutely, that's what I say, emphatically.'

Well then, Meletus, by those very gods we're talking about, make things even clearer than you have so far, both to me and to the jurymen here. I'm unable to establish whether you're saying I teach the young to believe that there are gods of some sort (in which case I believe there are gods myself, so that I'm not a total atheist; I'm innocent on that score), just different ones, not the ones the city believes in – I'm unclear whether *that*'s what you're charging me with, believing in different gods, or whether your charge is unqualified on both counts: that I don't myself believe in gods at all, and that this is what I teach others.

'This is what I'm saying, that you're a total non-believer in the gods.'

Meletus, my dear man, why on earth are you saying

that? Don't I suppose the sun, even, or the moon to be gods, then, like the rest of mankind?

'I swear to Zeus he doesn't, men of the jury, because he says the sun is a rock and the moon is made of earth.'

Do you suppose you're prosecuting Anaxagoras, my dear Meletus? Are you so contemptuous of these people here, and think them so illiterate as not to know that these assertions are bursting out of Anaxagoras' books? Are the young really supposed to be learning things from me that sometimes they'd be able to pick up from the orchestra for a drachma at the very most? Wouldn't they laugh at Socrates if he should ever pretend they were his and not Anaxagoras', especially when they're so strange? By Zeus, is that really how you think of me? You think I don't believe in any god at all?

'None at all, by Zeus; none whatsoever.'

You're not credible, Meletus, and in this instance I don't think you even believe yourself. Men of Athens, this person here seems to me totally insolent and unscrupulous; that's all that lies behind this indictment of his – a kind of youthful insolence and lack of scruple. He's like someone who's putting together a riddle, to see if I'll get the point: 'Will Socrates,

who's so wise, see that I'm making a joke of contradicting myself, or will I bamboozle him and the rest
of those listening?' For in fact he does appear to me
to be contradicting himself in the indictment: it's as
if he were saying, 'Socrates is guilty of not believing
in gods, but believing in gods.' Someone who says
that is merely playing about and not serious.

So let me explain to you, Athenians, why I take him
to be saying this. You, Meletus, answer my questions;
meanwhile I ask you, the jury, to remember the request
I made to you at the beginning of my defence, not to
protest if I express myself in my habitual style.

Is there anyone on earth, Meletus, who believes in
the existence of human things, but not in the existence of humans? I demand that the man answer,
Athenians, instead of making one protest after
another. Is there anyone who doesn't believe in
horses, but does believe in horsey things? Or doesn't
believe pipers exist, but does believe in piperish
things? There's no such person, Meletus, best of men;
if you won't give the answer, I'll say it for you, and
for these people here. At least answer the next question: is there anyone who believes in the existence of
divine things, but not in the existence of divinities?

'There's no one.'

How good of you to answer – even if you could barely get the words out, and because the jury here forced you to. Well then: you say that I both believe and teach that there are divine things, whether these are new ones or old ones – for the moment I don't mind; at any rate, on your account I do believe in divine things, and you've sworn to precisely that in your indictment of me. But if I believe in divine things, then surely there's no way I can avoid believing in divinities? Isn't that so? It is; since you don't reply, I'll put you down as agreeing with me. And divinities – don't we suppose these either actually to be gods, or at any rate children of gods? Do you agree or not?

'Yes, absolutely.'

Fine: so if in fact I believe in divinities, as you yourself claim I do, then if divinities are some sort of gods, that'll be the riddle I'm saying you're putting together, as your way of making a joke, that while I don't believe in gods, then again I do believe in gods, given that I believe in divinities; if on the other hand these divinities are only the children of gods, whether bastards of some sort, or born from nymphs, or whoever it is they're said to be from, who on earth would believe in children of gods and not in gods? It would be just as strange as if someone were to believe in the offspring of mares and donkeys, namely mules, but didn't believe there were mares or donkeys. When you composed your indictment like this, Meletus, it *must* have been to see if we'd get the joke – or else it was because you were at a loss as to what true crime you could charge me with. If you're seriously proposing to convince anyone with even a bit of intelligence *both* that someone who believes in divine things must also believe in things to do with gods *and* that this same person won't believe in divinities, or gods, or heroes – well, there's no way you can possibly convince anyone at all.

[*The cross-examination of Meletus ends.*]

So there you are, men of Athens. To show that I'm not guilty according to the terms of Meletus' indictment doesn't seem to me to require much from me; just the little I've offered is enough. But believe you me, there's no mistake about my earlier claim. I've earned myself a lot of hatred, and from a lot of people, and this is what will convict me, if that's how it turns out: not Meletus, and not Anytus either, but the malicious slander of people in general. That's taken down many others before me, good men too, and I imagine it'll take more; there's no danger it will end with me.

Well, probably someone will say to me, 'Then aren't you ashamed of yourself, Socrates, for going in for the kind of activity that puts you in the danger you're in now, of being put to death?' To this person I'll retort, and justly, 'You're wrong, my man, if you think a person who's of any use at all should take danger into account, weighing up his chancces of living or dying, instead of making it the sole consideration, whenever he acts, whether his actions are just or unjust, and whether they're what a good man would do or a bad one. By your reasoning all those demi-gods who died at Troy would be poor creatures; not least the son of Thetis, who was so contemptuous of danger when he compared it with incurring disgrace that when his mother, a goddess, addressed him, eager as he was to kill Hector – with words that were I imagine something like this: "Son, if you take revenge for the killing of your friend Patroclus, and kill Hector, you'll prepare your own death; for straightway," the poet says, "after Hector's is your death prepared" – when he heard this, he looked down on death and danger and, having much greater fear of living a coward and not avenging those he loved, the poet has him saying, "Then straightway let me die, with the guilty punished; or here shall I lie, an object of mirth beside the beaked ships, a dead weight upon earth." Surely you don't think *he* cared about death and danger?'

That's how it is, men of Athens, in truth: wherever a person makes his stand, either because that's where he thinks it best for him to be or under orders from a superior, that, it seems to me, is where he must stay and face danger, taking nothing into account, even death, before avoiding what is shameful. I myself would have been behaving in a shocking fashion, men of Athens, if I stood firm, like everyone else, and risked death when the commanders you chose to command me gave me the order to do so, whether at Potidaea or Amphipolis or Delium, but then, when the god gave me my orders, as I thought and supposed he had, to live a life of philosophy, examining myself and others, at *that* point I conceived a fear either of death or of whatever else it might be and abandoned my post. It would indeed be a shocking thing to do, and would truly give someone just cause for taking me to court for not believing in the gods; after all, there I'd be, disobeying the oracle, fearing death and thinking I was wise when I wasn't. For I tell you, Athenians, the fear of death is simply this, thinking yourself wise when you are not; it's thinking you know what you don't know. Death may even be the greatest of all good things for a human being – no one knows, yet people fear it as if they knew for sure that it's the greatest of bad things. And how is this kind of ignorance not reprehensible – thinking one knows what one doesn't? As for me, Athenians, it's just in this one respect that I probably am superior to the majority of mankind; if there's any way in which I'd claim to be wiser than the next man, it would be because, not possessing enough knowledge about the things in Hades, I actually think I don't know; whereas I do know that to be guilty of disobeying someone better than me, whether god or man, is bad and shameful. So, faced as I am with bad things that I know to be bad, I'll never turn tail for fear of things that, for all I know, may even be good. So now imagine you're prepared to let me go, and refuse to listen to Anytus, who said that either I shouldn't have been brought to court in the first place or, since I have been brought here, it was not an option not to apply the death penalty – because, he said, if I get off, your sons will all set about doing what Socrates teaches and all be totally corrupted: imagine that you said to me, in response to this, 'Socrates, for the moment we're not going to listen to Anytus, and we're prepared to let you go, but on this one condition, that you stop spending your time in this search of yours, and you stop doing philosophy. But if you're caught doing this in the future, we'll put you to death.' Well, my point was that, if you let me go on these conditions, I'd say to you, 'I have the greatest respect and love for you, men of Athens, but I shall obey the god rather than you, and so long as I breathe and so long as I am able I shall never stop doing philosophy, exhorting you all the while and declaring myself to whichever of you I meet – saying the sort of things that it's my habit to say: "Best of men, I ask you this: when you're an Athenian, and so belong to the greatest city, the one with the highest reputation for wisdom and strength, aren't you ashamed of caring about acquiring the greatest possible amount of money, together with reputation and honours, while not caring about, even sparing a thought for, wisdom and truth, and making your soul as good as possible?" And every time one of you disputes the matter with me and claims that he *does* care, I won't let him get away with it and walk away. Instead I'll question and examine and challenge him, and if he doesn't seem to me to have acquired excellence, but claims that he has, I'll rebuke him for making things that are most valuable his lowest priority and giving higher priority to things of lesser worth. That's what I'll do for any one of you I meet, whether young or old, foreigner or citizen – though I put my fellow citizens first, insofar as you are more akin to me. This is what the god tells me to do, make no mistake about it, and I don't think you've ever yet benefited more from anything than you have from my service to the god. What I *do*, as I move around among you, is just this: I try to persuade you, whether younger or older, to give less priority, and devote less zeal, to the care of your bodies or of your money than to the care of your soul and trying to make it as good as it can be. What I say to you is: "It's not from money that excellence comes, but from excellence money and the other things, all of them, come to be good for human beings, whether in private or in public life." So if it's by saying *this* that I corrupt the young, it will be this that is damaging them; and if anyone claims that I say something other than this, they're talking nonsense. So, men of Athens,' I'd say to you, 'that's what you need to take into account when you make your decision either to do what Anytus says or not – either let me go or don't, knowing that I would behave no differently even if that meant I'd be put to death many times over.'

Don't protest, men of Athens, but keep to the terms of my request to you, to hear me out and not protest at anything I say, because I think you'll benefit if you do listen. In any case I'm now going to say more things that probably will have you shouting out at me; just don't do it. What you should know is that if I'm the sort of person I say I am, your killing me will do me less damage than it does you; for neither will Meletus damage me, nor Anytus – nor could he, since I think it's not permitted for a better man to be damaged by a worse one. He'll have me killed, no doubt, or sent into exile, or stripped of my citizenship, and probably – I imagine he isn't alone in this – he thinks of these as great evils; but that's not how I think of them. I think it a much worse thing to be doing what he's now doing, trying to have a man put to death without just cause. So as a matter of fact, men of Athens, far from defending myself, as one might suppose, what I'm doing now is actually defending *you*, so that you don't make a mistake with the god's gift to you by casting your votes against me. Because if you do put me to death, you

won't easily find anyone else quite like me, attached
by the god to the city, if it's not too comic an image,
as if to a horse – a big and noble horse, but one that's
rather sleepy because of its size, all the time needing
to be woken up by some sort of gadfly: this is the kind
of role the god gave me when he attached me to the
city, and the result is that there's never a moment when
I'm not waking you up and cajoling and rebuking you,
each one of you, the whole day long, settling on you
wherever you may be. Another one like me, Athenians,
as I say, it won't be easy for you to find, and if you take
my advice you'll spare me; but probably you'll be
irritated at me, and like people who are woken up as
they're nodding off you'll hit out at me, taking Anytus'
advice instead of mine, and take the easy course of
putting me to death, after which you'll spend the rest
of your lives asleep, unless in his care for you the god
should send someone else to stop you. That I really
am the sort of person to have been given by the god
to the city you might infer from something about me
that doesn't look quite human: that I've totally neglected my own affairs, and put up with the neglect of
what belongs to me for so many years now, while
always acting in your interest, approaching each of

you privately as if I were a father or elder brother and trying to persuade you to care for excellence. That would be a reasonable way for me to behave, if I made something out of it, and got paid for my exhortations, but as it is you can see for yourselves that, while my accusers show no sense of shame in anything else they say about me, in this one respect they weren't able to brazen it out and provide a single witness to say that I ever either received or asked for payment. I offer my poverty as witness that I'm telling the truth; that should be enough.

Now it will probably seem strange that I go about as I do, busying myself with giving advice in private but not venturing to advise the city in public, when you're gathered together in the Assembly. The cause of this is something that you yourselves have often heard me talking about, all over the place, that some god or 'divinity' intervenes with me – something Meletus caricatured in his indictment. It's something that started in my boyhood, a sort of voice that comes to me and, when it comes, always discourages me from doing what I'm about to do, never encourages me. It's this that opposes my playing the statesman, and it's a fine thing that it does, it seems to me, for you can be quite sure, men of Athens, that if I'd set about a political career all those years ago, I'd long ago have come to a sticky end and would have been of no use either to you or to myself. Don't be annoyed with me for telling the truth: there isn't anyone in the world who'll survive if he genuinely opposes you or any other popular majority and tries to prevent widespread injustice and lawlessness from occurring in the city. Anyone who's really fighting for justice must live as a private citizen and not as a public figure if he's going to survive even a short time.

What I'll offer you as evidence for all this is not just words but the hard facts that you set such store by. You've heard the details of my history, which show you that fear of death will not make me give in to anything or anyone if it means going against what's just; I'll even die not giving in. What I'm going to mention to you is vulgar, the sort of thing that's typically talked about in court cases, but all the same it's true. I've never in my life held any office in the city, men of Athens, except that I did serve as a member of the Council; and it happened that my tribe, Antiochis, held the presidency when you approved the proposal to put the ten generals who failed to pick up the dead from

35

the sea-battle on trial together – contrary to the law, as all of you decided later on. At the time, I alone among those presiding opposed your doing anything contrary to the laws and voted against; and when the orators were ready to move against me and have me taken away, with your loud support, I thought I should rather take my chances on the side of law and justice than be on your side, out of a fear of imprisonment or death, when you were approving things that were not just. This was during the time when the city was still ruled by the democracy; when the oligarchy was instituted, the Thirty had their go at me, sending for me and four others to come to the Roundhouse, and ordering us to bring Leon of Salamis from Salamis for execution; lots of other people found this sort of thing happening to them all the time, as the oligarchs gave out orders so as to spread responsibility for what was going on as widely as possible. Then it was that I showed not by mere talk but by my actions that the amount I care about dying – if it's not too boorish to say so – is zero, and that all my care is devoted to doing nothing unjust, or impious. The fact is that that regime, for all its power, did not terrify me into doing something that was unjust. Instead, when we left the

Roundhouse, the other four went off to Salamis and brought Leon in, but I went off home. I would probably have been executed for this if the regime hadn't been brought to an end shortly afterwards. You'll find plenty of witnesses for all of this.

So do you think I would have survived for so many years if I had taken a public role and performed it – as any good man should – as the ally of everything just, and making this, as it must be, the highest priority? Not by a long way, men of Athens; and no one else in the world would survive for long like that, either. But if I have ever performed any action in any public context, you'll find me exactly as I've described, and in private the same: someone who has never yet agreed to anything contrary to justice with anyone at all, and certainly not with any of those they slanderously call my pupils. I have never, ever, been anybody's teacher; if anyone, young or old, wants to listen to me as I talk and do what I do, I've never begrudged it to anyone, nor do I talk to people if I get money for it but otherwise not. Instead, I offer myself to rich and poor alike, for them to ask their questions and, if anyone wishes, to listen to whatever I have to say and answer *my* questions. Whether any one of these people turns

37

out well or not, it wouldn't be fair for me to be held responsible for things that I never to this day promised anyone he'd learn from me, and have never taught, and if anyone says he ever learned or heard from me something in private of a sort that all the rest didn't hear as well, then you can be certain that he's not telling the truth.

Why is it, then, that some people enjoy spending large amounts of time with me? You have heard my explanation, men of Athens – and it's no less than the truth of the matter: that they enjoy witnessing the examination of people who think they're wise when they're not; and it has its delights. But what I do, as I say, I do because the god has assigned it to me, whether he communicates through oracular responses, or dreams, or any other means gods use to assign whatever task it may be to human beings.

And what I say, men of Athens, is both true and easily checked. Just think. If I'm currently corrupting some of the young, and I have corrupted others, then surely – let's suppose that some of them are now old enough to realize that I advised them badly in their youth: surely now is the time they should be stepping up and pressing charges by way of getting their own back? Or, if they were reluctant to do it themselves, shouldn't some of their relatives be stepping in, whether fathers, brothers, or whichever? If their kinsmen were the victims of some malfeasance on my part, shouldn't they now be mindful of it and pay me back? There are more than enough of them here: I can see them with my own eyes – first of all there's Crito, my coeval and fellow demesman, who's the father of Critobulus here; next there's Lysanias of Sphettus, father of Aeschines, and also Antiphon of Cephissus, Epigenes' father, both there with their sons; and then there are others whose brothers have spent their time with me, Nicostratus son of Theozotides, brother of Theodotus – admittedly, Theodotus is dead, so he couldn't have asked Nicostratus to act for him; Paralius too, son of Demodocus, whose brother was Theages; and there's Adimantus, son of Ariston, whose brother is Plato there, and Aiantodorus, whose brother is Apollodorus – also here. I can identify lots of others as well, one of whom Meletus should surely have offered you as a witness, preferably during his own speech; or if he forgot to do it then, let him do it now (I'll make him that concession), and let him say whether he has something like that up his sleeve. In fact you'll find it's quite the opposite. You'll find them all ready to help me, the corrupter, the one that's doing damage, or so Meletus and Anytus claim, to members of their family. It might perhaps be reasonable for those who've been corrupted to come to my aid themselves; but those who weren't corrupted, and are more grown up now, the relatives of those others – what reason do they have for coming to my aid except the one that's correct and just, that they know Meletus is lying and I'm telling the truth?

So there you are, Athenians; that's pretty much all I have to say in my defence, apart from some other things probably of the same sort. Perhaps one of you will take offence when he remembers how *he* behaved, if even when fighting a case less serious than the one I'm fighting he resorted to begging and supplicating the jury, in floods of tears, bringing his little children into court so that everyone should feel as sorry as anything for him, other relatives too, and lots of friends; and here I am, apparently proposing to do none of these things even when faced – so people will suppose – with the last and worst of all dangers. Perhaps these thoughts will cause one or another of you to harden his view of me; he'll get angry with me on these very grounds, and cast his vote accordingly. If any one of you is in this position – I don't think he should be, but in any case, if he is – I think it would be a decent response to him to say, 'Actually, best of men, even I have *relatives*, I imagine; this is that saying of Homer's – I'm not born "from oak or from rock", but from human beings, so that I do have relatives, and, yes, sons too, men of Athens, three of them, one by now a lad but the other two still small; all the same I will not bring any one of them into court and beg you to acquit me.' So *why* won't I do any of these things? Not out of wilfulness, men of Athens, nor out of disrespect for you; whether I face death with confidence or not is a different issue, but so far as appearances are concerned, doing any of the things in question would seem to me not to reflect well on me, or you, or the city as a whole, given my age and the name that I have – whether it's true or it's false, it's the established view that 'Socrates' is in some respect superior to the common run of mankind. Well, if those among you who are thought to excel in wisdom, or courage, or any other kind of excellence are going to behave like that, it'd be shameful; I've seen people doing it, when they're on trial – people who are thought to be of some worth, but then go on to do surprising things because they think something awful will be happening to them if they die, as if they'll be immortal providing *you* don't kill them off. People like that seem to me to hang a badge of shame on the city, so that a visitor might even suppose that those outstandingly excellent Athenians whom their fellow citizens choose over themselves for public offices and other kinds of honour are no better than women. Behaviour like that, men of Athens, is not only something you shouldn't indulge in yourselves, if you've any worth whatever in people's eyes, but if I indulge in it, you shouldn't let me; you should give a clear indication that you'll much sooner vote against someone who makes the city a laughing-stock by bringing on these pitiful exhibitions than against the man who keeps his peace.

But quite apart from the question of appearances, Athenians, it also doesn't seem to me just to *beg* a member of the jury, or to get off by begging. The just thing is to inform and convince. A juryman doesn't sit for the purpose of giving out justice as a favour, but to decide where justice lies; and he's sworn an oath that he won't dispense favours as he sees fit, but will make his decision according to the laws. Neither, then, should I try to get you into the habit of breaking your oath, nor should you acquire the habit, because then neither I nor you would be behaving piously. So, men of Athens, please don't expect me to behave towards you in ways that I don't think either honourable, or just, or pious, particularly and especially – Zeus! – when it's on a charge of impiety that I'm in the process of defending myself against Meletus here. Plainly, if I were to persuade you by begging, browbeating you when you're under oath, I'd turn out to be teaching *you* that the gods don't exist, and I'd literally be making it part of my defence to accuse myself of not believing in them. But that's not the case at all; I do believe in the gods, men of Athens, as none of my accusers does, and I leave it in your hands and in the god's to reach whatever decision about me is going to be best both for me and for you.

[*Socrates speaks again after the voting.*]

There are many reasons, men of Athens, why I'm not upset about what has occurred, and at your having voted against me, but the main reason is that it was not unexpected. In fact I'm much more surprised at the numbers of votes on the two sides. I didn't think the margin would be so small; I thought it would be a big one. As it is, it seems that if a mere thirty votes had gone the other way, I would have been acquitted. So far as Meletus' contribution is concerned, I think I actually do stand acquitted, even now, and not only that, it's obvious to anyone that if Anytus hadn't come forward to accuse me, and Lycon, Meletus would have been fined a thousand drachmas for not getting the required fifth of the votes.

In any case, the man proposes the penalty of death. Fine: what alternative penalty shall I put to you, men of Athens? Or is it clear – the one I deserve? What, then? What do I deserve to have done to me, or what fine do I deserve to pay, for the crime of not spending my life keeping to myself? What I have done is to turn my back on the things most people care about – money-making, managing a household, generalships, popular speech-making and all the other aspects of communal life in the city, whether public offices or private clubs and factions – because I concluded that I was truly too fair-minded a person to go in for this sort of thing and stay alive. So I didn't take that turning, because I knew that that way I would be no use at all either to you or to myself. Instead I headed along a different route, one that would lead, as I claim, to my doing you, privately, the greatest of good turns, as I try to persuade each one of you both to stop caring for your possessions before caring for yourself and making yourself as good and wise as possible, and to stop caring for the city's possessions before caring for the city itself – and to apply the same rule in the same way in caring for everything else. What, then, do I deserve to have happen to me, if that's the kind of person I am? Something good, I submit, men of Athens, if I'm to set my penalty in accordance with what I truly deserve, and not only that, the sort of good thing that would fit my case. So what does fit the case of a poor man who's your benefactor and needs free time to exhort you all? There's nothing that fits better, men of Athens, than to have such a person fed at public expense in the Prytaneum; much better him than one of you who's won a horse-race at Olympia, or won with a pair or a team of four, because someone like that makes you seem happy, whereas because of me you *are* happy, and what's more he doesn't need feeding and I do. So if I'm to make a just assessment of the penalty I deserve, this is it – free food in the Prytaneum.

Probably when I say this too I'll seem to you to be

talking in the same wilful sort of way as when I talked about the practice of making pitiful appeals. But it isn't like that, men of Athens; rather it's like this – I'm convinced that I wrong no one in the world, intentionally, but I don't convince you of it, because the time we've had for conversation between us is too short. In fact, in my opinion, if the law were the same here as everywhere else, and you had to spend not just one but several days judging capital cases, you would have been convinced; as it is, the slanders against me are too great to be undone in so short a time. In any case, given my conviction that I do no wrong to anyone, I'm hardly likely to go on to wrong myself by saying on my own account I deserve something bad and myself proposing that kind of penalty. Why would I do that? Out of fear? Fear of having done to me what Meletus proposes, when I say I don't know whether it's a good thing or a bad thing? Instead, then, am I to choose one of the things I know very well to be bad, proposing that as my penalty? Imprisonment, perhaps? Why, I ask you, should I live in prison, as the slave of whichever collection of people happened to make up the Eleven, year after year? A fine, then, and imprisonment until I pay it? It's the same answer I gave just now – I don't have any money to pay with. So what about my proposing exile – since probably you'd accept that? I'd have to be possessed with a great passion for life, men of Athens, to make me so poor at adding up that I couldn't do a simple calculation: when it was even beyond you, my fellow citizens, to put up with my discourses and arguments, how likely would it be that others would easily manage it? They were just too much for you, too hateful, so now you're setting out to be permanently rid of them; why should *others* put up with them? Of course I can work it out, men of Athens. A fine life it would be if I did leave Athens, a person of my age, moving on to one city after another and living the life of a fugitive. Because that's what it would be; I'm sure that wherever I go the young will listen to me talk as they do here. If I drive them away, they'll be the ones who'll persuade their elders to drive me out; and if I don't, their fathers and other relatives will drive me out on their account anyway.

Someone will probably say, 'But, Socrates, can't you live in exile without talking, just keeping your peace? Surely you can do that?' To convince some of you about this is the most difficult thing of all. If I say 'That would be to disobey the god; how *can* I keep my peace, then?', you'll not believe me because you'll think I'm dissembling; if on the other hand I say that it actually is the greatest good for a human being to get into discussion, every day, about goodness and the other subjects you hear me talking and examining myself and others about, and that for a human being a life without examination is actually not worth living – if I say that, you'll be even less convinced. But that's how I say it is, Athenians; it's just not easy to convince you.

At the same time, I'm not used to thinking I deserve anything bad at all. In fact if I'd had any money available, I'd propose a fine of whatever amount I'd be in a position to pay, since it wouldn't have done me any damage to pay it. But actually I don't have money – unless of course you're willing to set the penalty at what I *could* pay. I imagine I'd probably be able to find a mina of silver for you. So that's what I propose.
[*A message is passed from the audience.*]

One moment – Plato here, men of Athens, along with Crito and Critobulus and Apollodorus – they're telling me to propose thirty minae, with them as guarantors; so that's the amount I propose, and as

guarantors of the money these people will be credit-
worthy enough.

[*The sentence of death is approved; Socrates addresses the
court for the final time.*]

You'll not have bought a lot of time at this price,
men of Athens: getting the name – from anyone who
wants to abuse the city – for being the ones who killed
off 'Socrates, a wise man'. (People who want to find
fault with Athens will of course say that I'm wise even
if I'm not.) At any rate if you'd waited a little time,
you'd have had the same outcome without doing anything. You can see my age for yourselves, how far on
I am in life, how near to death. I say this not to all of
you, just to those of you who've voted to put me to
death. And I've got something else to say to these
people. You probably imagine, Athenians, that I stand
condemned because I lacked the sorts of arguments
with which I could have persuaded you, given always
that I supposed I should do and say everything to
escape the penalty. Far from it. If I've been condemned
for the lack of something, it's not a lack of arguments
but a lack of effrontery and shamelessness and the

49

willingness to address you in the sorts of ways that it'd please you most to hear – wailing and lamenting and doing and saying plenty of other things unworthy of me, as I claim, even if they're the sorts of things you're used to hearing from everyone else. I didn't think then that I should do anything unworthy of a free man, despite the danger I face, nor do I now regret having made my defence as I did. I'd far rather make that defence and die than demean myself and live. No one, whether it's in court or in war, whether it's myself or anyone else, should try to escape death by any means he can devise. In battles the opportunity is often there to avoid death by throwing away one's arms or turning to supplicate one's pursuers, and there are other devices for avoiding death in every sort of danger, if only one has the face to do and say anything no matter what. But I hazard, Athenians, that the difficult thing is not to avoid death; more difficult is avoiding viciousness, because viciousness is a faster runner than death. So now, because I'm so slow and old, I've been caught by the slower runner, but because they're so quick and clever my accusers have been caught by the quicker one; and if I'm going to leave the court condemned by you to death, *they* will leave it convicted by truth of depravity and injustice. They accept their penalty as I do mine. I suppose it's probably how it had to be, and I think it's a fair result.

The next thing I want to do is to make a prophecy to you, the ones who voted against me; I'm now at that moment when human beings are most prone to turn prophet, when they're about to die. I tell you, you Athenians who have become my killers, that just as soon as I'm dead you'll meet with a punishment that – Zeus knows – will be much harsher than the one you've meted out to me by putting me to death. You've acted as you have now because you think it'll let you off being challenged for an account of your life; in fact, I tell you, you'll find the case quite the opposite. There'll be more, not fewer, people challenging you – people that I was holding back, without your noticing it, and they'll be all the harsher because they're younger, and you'll be crosser than you are now. If you think killing people will stop anyone reproaching you for not living correctly, you're not thinking straight. Being let off like that is not only quite impossible, it's the opposite of fine; the finest and easiest kind of letting off is when, instead of trying to cut other people down to size, each of you takes the measures needed to make yourself as good as you can be. So that's the prophecy I leave behind for those who voted to condemn me.

As for those of you who voted for me, I'll be happy to talk to you about this thing that's happened to me, just while the court authorities are busy and before I go off to the place where I'm to go and die. [*Some of the jury are making to leave.*] Do stay, Athenians, just for those few moments, because there's nothing to stop us having a good talk to each other while we can. You're my friends, and I do want to show you what this thing that's now happened to me actually signifies. Men of the jury (because 'jurymen' is the correct name to give you), I've something striking to report to you. In all my time before now that accustomed prophetic ability of mine, the one I get from my 'divinity', was always with me, intervening again and again and opposing me in quite small matters, if ever I were to be going to act incorrectly in some respect. And now things have turned out for me as you yourselves observe, in a way that might be thought, and people actually think, the worst that can happen to anyone; but the god's sign failed to oppose either my leaving my house at dawn, or my coming up here to the court, or my saying anything I was going to say at any point in my speech. And yet on other occasions when I've been talking it has held me back all over the place in mid-speech; now, in relation to this whole business it has nowhere opposed my doing or saying anything. What do I suppose to be the reason for this? I'll tell you: it's because this thing that's happened has very likely been good for me. There's no way that those of us who think dying is a bad thing can be right; and I've had a powerful indication of that – there's no way that my accustomed sign wouldn't have opposed me if I wasn't going to do something good.

Let us look at things in the following way too, to see how great a hope there is that it's a good thing. Death is one or the other of two things: either the dead are nothing, as it were, and have no perception of anything, or else, as some people say, death is really a kind of change, a relocation of the soul from its residence here to another place. Now if the dead perceive nothing, but are as it were asleep, as when a sleeper sees nothing even in dreams, death would be a striking gain; for I imagine that if anyone had to pick out the night in which he'd slept so soundly as not even to see a dream and compare not just all other nights but the days of his life with that night – if he had to say, after thinking about it, how many days and nights in his life he'd lived through better and more pleasantly than *this* night, I imagine that not just any private individual but the Great King himself would find these days and nights easy to count by comparison with those other, dreamless ones; so that if death is something like that, I myself count it a gain, since from that perspective there'll be no difference between a single night and the whole of time. If on the other hand death is a kind of change of residence from here to another place, and what we're told is true, that all who have died are there, what greater good could there be, men of the jury? For if any new arrival in Hades, who has got away from those who call themselves judges here, will find himself before the true judges who are said to sit in judgement there, Minos, Rhadamanthus, Aeacus and Triptolemus, and those other demi-gods who became just in their own life, would that be a poor destination to move to? And what would any of you give to get together with Orpheus, or Musaeus, or Hesiod, or Homer? I'd happily die, myself, many times over if that's truly what awaits us, because I for one would pass the time wonderfully, when I met

Palamedes, or Ajax son of Telamon, or any such figure from the past, dead because of an unjust judgement – I'd be able to compare my experiences with theirs, and I think it'd be delightful enough; but the greatest thing is that I'd be able to spend my time examining people there and sniffing them out as I do people here, to see which of them is wise and which merely thinks he is but really isn't. What would one give, men of the jury, to examine the man who led that great army against Troy, or Odysseus, or Sisyphus, or – well, one could list countless others, women as well as men with whom it'd give immeasurable happiness to talk, to be with them and to examine them. People there certainly don't put one to death for it, I imagine; they're happier than people here in every respect, and especially because for the rest of time they are deathless, if indeed what we are told is true.

But you too, men of the jury, should be of good hope when you think of death, keeping the truth of this one thing in mind: that there is nothing bad that can happen to a good man whether in life or after he has died, nor are his affairs neglected by the gods. This business of mine now hasn't come about by accident; no, it's clear to me that it was *better* for me to die now and to be rid of life's ordinary business altogether. That's the reason why that sign of mine at no point turned me back, and why I'm not at all angry with those who voted against me, or with my accusers. All the same, that wasn't what was in their minds when they were voting against me and making their accusations. They did it thinking they were damaging me, and that's what they deserve to be blamed for. This much I ask of them: if my sons seem to you, when they reach puberty, to be caring about money or anything else before excellence, punish them, Athenians, by making them suffer in the very same way I used to make you suffer, and if they think they're something when they're not, reproach them as I have reproached you for not caring about the things they should and thinking they're something when they're not worth anything. If you do that, then I shall have had my just deserts from you, both for myself and for my sons.

But now it is time for us to leave: for me, to go to my death, and for you to go on living. Whether it's you or I who are going to a better thing is clear to no one but the god.